STORM BREAKERS

Silence the Storm of Depression

By

D.M. Samms, M.Th

© 2022 D.M. Samms

All rights reserved. No part of this book may be reproduced or used in any manner without the prior written permission of the copyright owner, except for the use of brief quotations in a book review.

To request permission, contact the author at info@stormbreakers.org

ISBN: 979-8-9858512-0-5

ISBN (Spanish): 979-8-9858512-1-2

For speaking engagements or more information, visit: www.stormbreakers.org

Acknowledgements

First and foremost, I must acknowledge my Lord and Savior Jesus Christ, without whom I am nothing. To Him be the glory, honor, and praise forever and ever. The chains were broken from my life at nineteen, but I didn't know how to accept His healing until much later. The patience, direction, and impartation by Christ into my life made this book – a personal and unlikely-to-achieve goal – a reality.

To my wife, who has had to endure the ups and downs, the ins and outs, the endless discussions and iterations of how to formulate the concepts in this book. Who has loved me, even when I could not love myself. Who stayed by my side as I struggled through enacting the concepts in this book. I am in love with you, Shalvah.

To my Bishop, who by God was used to help me walk through this life. Who believed in me when I could not, who saw with the eyes of Christ through my darkest hour, and who reminded me that with God, all things are possible. Including a wretch like me writing literature. God knew exactly what He was doing by placing me in your flock.

I owe a debt of gratitude to these three that I will never truly be able to repay, and without whom this book would have never come to fruition. Thank you, from the depths of my soul, for helping me accomplish a life-long dream.

Preface

My prayer for the reader:

My Lord God, Your majesty is eternal. You know no defeat. Your Word shall not return unto you void. Your enemies cannot triumph over You, neither do they have dominion over anything that You have not declared. In the name of Jesus Christ, I pray for all those who will receive a copy of this book.

For you who are fighting the good fight of faith against the invisible enemy of their own thoughts: I pray that mental torment ceases, now, even as you pick up this bundle of pages! I pray the spirit of heaviness drops off you, and that your burden lightens in a significantly noticeable way. I pray for mental clarity, that thought patterns be corrected, now, in the name of Jesus! I pray strongholds are cast down even as they turn these pages. I pray grace over them, a divine influence of the heart to perform the will of God, that they may defeat the enemy in their life, even cast Satan out of every work they put their hands to. I pray the power of Christ be revealed to them in a tangible way. I pray for perfect love to cast out *all* fear, in the mighty name of Jesus!

For those who will be serving someone struggling with depression: I pray discernment enters your spirit, now, in Jesus' name. I pray that clarity enters their being. A clarity which would minister that salvation in Jesus Christ, a belief in His Word, and submission to the Holy Ghost is enough to overcome the Devil and his devices. I pray unshakeable faith enters their being, now, to defend against the doubt that may rise up in the person they are ministering to, that they may inject into the struggling person's soul the simplicity of hope in

Christ that feels so impossibly far away for them. I pray a divine quickening over them, that they would be swift to pray, swift to listen, swift to empathize, swift to enact the Word of God.

My Lord, my Savior, My God, have Your way with this book and with all who would come upon it. In Jesus' name. Amen.

Table of Contents

Chapter 1 - Purpose Is…   11

Chapter 2 - God Is…   19

Chapter 3 - Depression Is…   29

Chapter 4 - Hope Is…   45

Chapter 5 - Appetite Is…   53

Chapter 6 - Defense Is…   65

Chapter 7 - Thought Is…   81

Chapter 8 - Cheese Is…   95

Chapter 9 - The W.E.S.T. Is…   107

Chapter 10 - Victory Is…   131

Chapter 1

Purpose Is…

Relief. I just wanted relief.

I'd entered into a time of prayer for just that purpose. Being in the presence of the Almighty is one of the few places where I can truly, honestly be who I am, without fear of judgment, without fear of repercussion. I might be in need of encouragement, I might need correction, or I might just need a good, healthy session of venting. But when I go before God, I can be naked and unafraid to take off *the mask*.

You know what I'm talking about.

Over and over again, you hear about people who suffer in silence, who have manufactured a way of operating in this world where they can hide the debilitating feelings and emotions behind a façade. They engage their "actor" mode. They put on their *mask* and appear normal, hold a job, maintain a relationship, maybe even raise a family. But under the outward appearance, there is great emotional turmoil stirring inside. For many, it's known as smiling depression.

"Hey, friend! How are you? Who, me? I'm ready for a nap, thanks for asking! No, I'm good. Just living the dream!"

For me, the mask was how I functioned. And even now, removing it is simultaneously liberating and scary, overwhelming and comforting. I know when

I seek out God, the mask has to come down. He wouldn't accept anything less. I often cry during worship. Maybe *blubber incessantly* is a better descriptor, even during joyful praise songs when others are dancing and shouting. I've learned to embrace it. Praise God for the church I attend, where I don't look *that* weird doing it!

I'd gotten to that all-too-familiar point where things were overwhelming again. Where the mask wasn't helping anymore and the despair of everyday life was leading me towards isolation. I knew I needed to feel the comfort of the Lord.

I wasn't searching for anything in particular during my prayer time that day. It was more of a supplication-type prayer, asking for His touch and His presence. I was struggling to see my value as a Christian. My career appeared to be actively deteriorating and fatherhood seemed impossible. I wanted nothing more than to be at peace. Just for a little while, anyways.

My heart, burdened by years of depressive and intrusive thoughts, was overwhelmed. But then, a simple sentence uttered in the still, small voice of God radiated within my being.

"Depression is an appetite."

Plain and direct. Softly spoken but firm in conviction. And, at that moment, I began to ponder what that might mean.

As someone who up until that point had dealt with depressive emotions throughout most of his life, it hit me hard in the chest. It was a juxtaposition of simplicity and complexity. And it was exactly what

I needed. So, enamored with the concept, I chewed on it for weeks.

Questions begat questions. What does this mean? What does appetite have to do with depression? Why is God telling me this? How do I apply this? I wanted healing and comfort, but this is what God shared with me? Why? And why me? How, exactly, do I seek healing from my Lord and Savior? More importantly, how do I *receive* healing from Him?

There must be millions of prayers to God for healing on a daily, if not hourly, basis. Earnest prayers born from struggle and pain, both physical and mental. Suffering that many of us could not even imagine. And so many are still hurting.

I had hit the proverbial wall. I didn't have an answer to those questions until God opened my understanding. And immediately, the purpose began to take root.

Mark 4:39

"And he arose, and rebuked the wind, and said unto the sea, Peace, be still. And the wind ceased, and there was a great calm."

This would be the beginning of my search to understand depression, learn how to silence my mind, and become a Storm Breaker.

Chapter 2

God Is…

The Bible is a remarkable book, in every sense of the word. In it lies prophecies and historical accounts, wisdom and wonder, foolish men and spiritual forces. Surely there is no other compilation of writings that compare. And how could any man-made creation compare to divinely inspired scripture? The Bible witnesses itself:

1 Timothy 3:16

"All scripture is given by inspiration of God, and is profitable for doctrine, for reproof, for correction, for instruction in righteousness."

2 Peter 1:16

"For we have not followed cunningly devised fables, when we made known unto you the power and coming of our Lord Jesus Christ, but were eyewitnesses of his majesty."

1 Thessalonians 2:13

"For this cause also thank we God without ceasing, because, when ye received the word of God which ye heard of us, ye received it not as the word of men, but as it is in truth, the word of God, <u>which effectually worketh also in you that believe.</u>"

The Word of God is full of reinforcements of the inerrancy of scripture. And it also has many caveats and warnings to the reader. But there is one in particular that must be established for all of the concepts discussed within these pages to be effective when put into practice.

Hebrews 11:6

"But without faith it is impossible to please him: for he that cometh to God must believe that <u>he is</u>, and that he is a rewarder of them that diligently seek him."

In the context of this book, it is of utmost importance that you understand, *and believe*, that scripture. Millions, if not billions, of people have read the Bible, engaged its wording and descriptions, smudging the ink of its pages on their fingers. But just as the Bible says that many are called and few are chosen, the same can be said for those that truly believe. Many have interacted with the Word, but few have truly believed in the power of the Word. Hebrews 11:6 says that when we come to God, we must believe that He is.

Full stop.

He is…real. He is…faithful. He is…omnipotent. He is…omniscient. All necessary components to the character of God.

The caveat in this scripture is that rewards (results) are contingent upon belief. God is, without a doubt, a rewarder of them that diligently seek Him, just as the scripture points out. But if our ultimate goal is healing, and not to enter into and maintain a relationship with Jesus Christ, then our faith is in vain.

As Matthew 6:33 says so succinctly:

"*But seek ye first the kingdom of God, and his righteousness; and all these things shall be added unto you.*"

If I am not seeking Jesus and looking to fulfill all that is required of the believer, expecting "*all these things*" to be added to me will be an exercise in frustration.

As a Christian, I decided a long time ago that whether I would be healed or not, I would serve Jesus. Paraphrasing Matthew 18, it's better to enter into Heaven unhealed, than to enter into Hell full-bodied.

Healing on this temporary plane of existence would be a side victory, if it came at all. But making Heaven, and spending eternity in the presence and warmth and light of God Almighty... That is true victory. Jesus is enough for me. And since I was serving Him, I concluded that I might as well work the principles of the Word of God and receive my healing.

Over this entire process I have come to appreciate that James, writing in the second chapter of his epistle, was right: faith without works is dead. Faith causes evidence of itself to pour out of the one possessing it. If there is no evidence, then how can I say I have faith? And I would argue that the inverse is logically appropriate and applicable as well: works without faith are irrelevant.

Performing the actions in this book may benefit you because they are founded and supported by biblical principles. You may even find temporary relief from turmoil and temptation. But the Holy Ghost is searching the depths of our souls for belief in Jesus

Christ, without which the lasting, transformative power you are seeking will not manifest in your life.

1 John 5:10-11
"¹⁰He that believeth on the Son of God hath the witness in himself: he that believeth not God hath made him a liar; because he believeth not the record that God gave of his Son.
¹¹And this is the record, that God hath given to us eternal life, and this life is in his Son."

Ephesians 1:19
"And what is the exceeding greatness of his power to us-ward who believe, according to the working of his mighty power."

If you haven't already done so, please surrender your life to Jesus Christ. Ask Him to shepherd over you, to guide you, ask Him to be born again, as it says in John 3:3. Seek him diligently.

I would also strongly encourage you who are already believers to consider this scripture:

> 2 Corinthians 13:5
> *"Examine yourselves, whether ye be in the faith; prove your own selves. Know ye not your own selves, how that Jesus Christ is in you, except ye be reprobates?"*

We are commanded by scripture to examine ourselves and our actions. All too often, we aren't really, honestly examining our faith. Instead, we are questioning ourselves, whether we *should* be in the faith or not. And there is a huge difference between those two actions.

In this context, to examine means to look for shortcomings honestly and without reservation and then to implement solutions. To question means to seek a way to escape or disprove our faith, and make invalid the necessity of salvation, reinforcing unbelief.

So I encourage you, brothers and sisters, examine with God's eyes, with His Word. And comport to it. Be honest with yourself. Biblically, Jesus said it this way:

Mark 1:15b
"Repent ye, and believe the gospel."

Chapter 3

Depression Is…

There are far too many preconceived notions surrounding depression. Some right, many more wrong, but ultimately, it's difficult to pin down what it really is, to fairly, neatly wrap it up in a pretty bow for easy consumption.

Here is one of the better definitions I could find:

"Depression is the state of being that negatively affects how you feel, the way you think, and how you act."

But as anyone who has suffered from depression knows, it is anything but fair, neat, or presented with a pretty bow. Depression is dark and messy. There are hot tears and suppressed fears, overwhelming thoughts and blinding negativity. And not to be overlooked is the exhaustion and lack of motivation. There is an inherent loneliness built into it, because people may not understand. Putting words to the situation takes too much effort. Or, worse yet, people see your struggle and *falsely* assume you are weak or lazy.

And all these are important to recognize, because often in those moments, you feel you are the only one who has ever experienced them – these feelings being the farthest thing from the truth. Studies show that upwards of 280 million people worldwide struggle with depression (World Health Organization, 2021)!

When God so gently uttered into my soul that depression is an appetite, I heard the individual words, but I lacked the understanding of what they truly meant as a whole. So I determined to start seeking out definitions. And the definition about our state of being negatively affecting the sufferer sincerely lacked in detail the depth of the struggle I was experiencing.

Have a look at the symptoms as defined in the Diagnostic and Statistical Manual of Mental Disorders (DSM-5):

1. Depressed mood: For children and adolescents, this can also be an irritable mood.

2. Diminished interest or loss of pleasure in almost all activities.

3. Significant weight change or appetite disturbance: For children, this can be failure to achieve expected weight gain.

4. Sleep disturbance (insomnia or hypersomnia).

5. Psychomotor agitation or retardation (slow thinking and corresponding body movements).

6. Fatigue or loss of energy.

7. Feelings of worthlessness.

8. Diminished ability to think or concentrate; indecisiveness.

9. Recurrent thoughts of death, recurrent suicidal ideation without a specific plan, or a suicide attempt or specific plan for dying by suicide.

According to the DSM-5, these symptoms must be experienced over a two-week period, and while you need not experience them all, number two on the list is a required factor in considering depression as a diagnosis.

If I'm being forthcoming, I've experienced all of the above from an early age. My first memory of struggling with suicide was in the second grade. Many people believe that depression only affects certain demographics or is rooted in some kind of trauma. But the truth is, depression is no respecter of persons. It can affect anyone, often with no particular causal event.

The number of reasons why someone suffers from depression equals the number of those who suffer from it. Biological, hereditary, psychological, social, and spiritual backgrounds all factor into whether someone will experience symptoms of depression.

I want to take a brief side journey here and address the common belief that depression is solely a chemical imbalance. I came across an article by Amanda Efthimiou titled "Are We Over-Medicalizing Human Emotion?" (2019). In the article, Amanda describes a situation with a friend named Nadiya (not her real name). Nadiya had moved across the country to pursue her career shortly after graduating college.

While away, her mother was diagnosed with ovarian cancer. Nadiya agonized whether to return home, but her mother encouraged her to stay and pursue her career. Unexpectedly, her mother passed away just four months later.

This led to overwhelming feelings of guilt and eventually transitioned into full-blown symptoms of depression. Nadiya was encouraged by a friend to see a psychiatrist, where she revealed the extent of what she was experiencing. In the span of thirty-five minutes, the psychiatrist had diagnosed her with major depressive disorder – a much weightier and longer-term diagnosis than a major depressive "episode" – and immediately prescribed her antidepressant medication.

After reading that, I was utterly in shock at how quickly medication was prescribed. Between 2005 and 2008, there was a 400% increase in antidepressant usage in the United States (Juergens, 2021). Over-medicalizing indeed.

And this is just one instance of a societal behavior that manifests itself all too often. As opposed to helping this person process the perfectly normal, acceptable human feelings of regret and shame I assume Nadiya was experiencing, she was offered a pill. The use of medication to alter thinking patterns is like a two-edged sword. It may cut away at the problem, but it can lead to many more complications, some possibly worse than what was being experienced.

Oftentimes, I believe psychiatrists prescribe medications with the intent to stabilize their patient and address the emotional aspect after the chemical equilibrium is better restored.

A noble gesture, to be sure.

That decision, however, ignores the consequences of tampering with the organic composition in the brain.

It forces the brain, which is assumed to already be in a state of imbalance, to further alter the chemical configuration it is currently producing to address the newly introduced medicine.

Here is a very simplistic example. Let's say a hypothetical friend of ours, Gina, is experiencing a lack of motivation and a depressed mood. As you may know, the brain produces the neurotransmitter serotonin, which is influential in every part of our body, including motor skills and emotions.

Using an arbitrary number, let's say that Gina's brain needs ten molecules of serotonin to operate efficiently, but is only producing six. Gina goes to a psychiatrist, who prescribes Prozac, which will introduce enough serotonin to return to a healthy level of ten. Because her brain is operating with the understanding of only needing six, it reduces serotonin production down to two, to offset the sudden increase in the neurotransmitter (Whitaker, 2010). Thus a second imbalance is created, but this one is artificial.

Because Gina is not responding to the medication as she expects, she revisits the psychiatrist, who will have to adjust her prescription several times to get the right balance. Gina's brain will hopefully adjust to the new artificial levels in a healthy manner each time.

But, if the brain stops producing serotonin because it is being introduced artificially, what happens when Gina is no longer taking her medication? In a perfect world, the brain is able to, and will, restore the balance to the proper levels.

But that is not always the case. Many times, because the chemical in question is being introduced artificially, the brain will cease production, thereby causing a dependency to develop. It's a long, arduous, and dangerous process that I believe is enacted too often and too nonchalantly.

This is not to say that medication is unnecessary. On the contrary, there are scenarios where medication certainly may be required. But it is my belief that it should not be our primary mode of addressing these problems, nor can it be the ultimate be-all and end-all. Emotions are a part of the human experience and need to be felt and processed healthily, promoting mental resilience that this generation is struggling to obtain. Surely there is a better way than an Orwellian soma pill.

And there is. Enter the Word of God.

Remember King Saul after he sinned at Gilgal (*1 Samuel 16*). The Lord sent an evil spirit to torment him. While we clearly have reference in scripture to show that demonic oppression is real, not all affliction is because of sin. We can see this in action by reading this scripture:

John 9:1-2

"¹And as Jesus passed by, he saw a man which was blind from his birth.
²And his disciples asked him, saying, Master, who did sin, this man, or his parents, that he was born blind?"

The disciples made a judgment that either the blind man or his parents had sinned, and thus opened himself up to affliction. The consequence of this, in their opinion, left the man blind. But what did Jesus say in response?

John 9:3
"Jesus answered, Neither hath this man sinned, nor his parents: but that the works of God should be made manifest in him."

Jesus was challenging the disciples' thought process to not focus on the cause, but rather the purpose. Yes, even in struggle, even in depression, man can have purpose and glorify God. This is confirmed throughout scripture.

In fact, every vessel God used, apart from Jesus, was broken in one manner or another. Moses was a coward and a murderer; David an adulterous murderer; Peter denied Christ three times. They were all humans who were walking through this world imperfectly. But look at who they became. Moses was used to deliver the entire nation of Israel and was chosen to deliver the system of worship practiced by the Jews today. David was the apple of God's eye, an archetype of Christ, writing the book of Psalms and manifesting an example of repentance. Peter is known as the Rock, the foundation the church was built on.

What all of these examples (and there are many, many others) have in common is one particular factor: they came into contact with the Living God and were obedient to what He told them. To simplify, their encounter with the Lord changed the way those individuals believed, which changed the way they thought and acted.

If we are desirous of change in our lives, then the answer is the same whether we believe depression stems from a chemical imbalance, a spiritual oppression, neither, or both: an encounter with Jesus Christ. He can both heal a chemical imbalance and cast out the devil. He can change minds and heal hearts, molding the intangible parts of man that no one else can.

Chapter 4

Hope Is…

We must first understand then, that the goal of depression is to attack the biblical principle of hope in those under its oppression.

What do I mean?

You've probably seen those signs and stickers everywhere: "Faith, Hope, Love." But this is what the scripture says:

1 Corinthians 13:13

"And now abideth faith, hope, charity, these three; but the greatest of these is charity."

What these principles represent is very consequential and necessary to the believer.

Charity, or love, is the greatest of these because it manifested in the death and resurrection of Jesus Christ. He opened the door to salvation and gave access to the Father to all that would believe.

John 3:16

"For God so loved the world, that he gave his only begotten Son, that whosoever believeth in him should not perish, but have everlasting life."

Romans 5:8

"But God commendeth his love toward us, in that, while we were yet sinners, Christ died for us."

By this act of charity, all the gifts that God has reserved for mankind also became accessible: eternity in Heaven, redemption from sin, deliverance, healing, power over the Devil, prophecy, and so much more.

By this pure sacrifice of a blameless man, hope was also manifested to mankind. This hope allows us, as individuals, to believe that access to salvation and those spiritual gifts are available.

That a wretch like me could be cleansed and made whole by a Holy God. It opens our eyes to the very real future promised to us by scripture.

Romans 8:24

"**For we are saved by hope**: *but hope that is seen is not hope: for what a man seeth, why doth he yet hope for?*"

Psalm 42:5

"Why art thou cast down, O my soul? and why art thou disquieted in me? **hope thou in God**: for I shall yet praise him for the help of his countenance."

1 John 3:2-3

"²Beloved, now are we the sons of God, and it doth not yet appear what we shall be: but we know that, when he shall appear, we shall be like him; for we shall see him as he is.
³And every man that hath **this hope in him purifieth himself**, even as he is pure."

Finally, faith is the component that reaches into the future, grabs the promises of victory and healing we receive at Heaven's gates, and brings it back to the present moment, making those future promises tangible, effective, and actionable *now*.

Hebrews 11:1

"Now faith is the substance of things hoped for, the evidence of things not seen."

Hebrews 4:2

*"For unto us was the gospel preached, as well as unto them: but the word preached did not profit them, **not being mixed with faith** in them that heard it."*

If you have ever taken a fire safety course, you are probably familiar with the Fire Triangle and its elements: heat, oxygen, and fuel. When they combine, a chemical reaction happens, and fire ignites. Extinguish one part, and fire cannot exist.

Each of the three scriptural components – faith, hope, and charity – are necessary for salvation in Jesus Christ and to partake of all the gifts God has promised to us on Earth. Take away any of them, and we no longer have access to redemption.

If charity is removed, then Christ would not have died for us and salvation would not be possible.

If hope is broken, then we cannot see that salvation is available to us. Our belief is in vain; we walk this walk for no reason. There is no deliverance to us.

And if faith is missing, then we cannot please God, nor can we enter into eternal life. We cannot bring back those heavenly promises to overcome present struggles.

This is why depression is so dangerous and why the Devil is afflicting so many with it. It is an attack on the biblical principle of hope.

Put a little more succinctly, the scriptures say this:

Proverbs 13:12

"Hope deferred maketh the heart sick: but when the desire cometh, it is a tree of life."

This burden of hopelessness, of feeling like it will never be better, like nothing will ever work out, like there is no salvation, is a lie. The heart is sick. It's under siege, waves and wind battering against it. The sun is hidden behind endless gray skies and torrential rains. The storm is raging and dampening an integral component of the Christian walk.

The truth is, there is hope, there is salvation; and Jesus is *the* way, *the* truth, and *the* life we have been earnestly waiting for.

Chapter 5

Appetite Is…

When God said to me, "Depression is an appetite," did God mean that depression makes you hungry? Simplistic, to be sure, but it was one of my first attempts at understanding this concept.

I learned from the DSM-5 that overeating is one of the symptoms, but so is undereating (American Psychiatric Association, 2013). So that was ruled out rather quickly.

As I searched it out in the Spirit, He made it plain that He wasn't addressing the varied intricacies between filet mignon and Taco Bell. Appetite is a term used to describe a strong desire that has developed due to a pre-disposed preference or a regularly repeated behavior or mentality. God was speaking about negative behaviors that are detrimental to the individual.

In other words, an appetite is a precursor for an addiction.

Often associated with illicit drug or alcohol use, addiction is not solely limited to these behaviors. It is an outward manifestation of an inward struggle. The particular external substance one is addicted to can vary, but the corresponding behavior that is produced is almost identical: an intoxication that requires increasingly detrimental repetition.

Gluttony is viewed as an addiction to food. Pornography, often referred to as the new drug, has proven to be an addiction for millions of both men and women.

Even more worrisome, many things that seem to be innocent have been defined by society as addictive in nature. How many times have you heard someone say that they cannot even speak to people, let alone start their day without a cup of coffee? Or that they can't stop taking selfies or put down their social media feed?

I have even read articles on people who are addicted to shopping at Costco, the warehouse giant where anything from five-gallon tubs of mayonnaise to outdoor furniture to video game consoles and jewelry can be had (Lewis, 2016). These individuals have begun to brand themselves as "Costcoholics." Many have a compulsion to shop there two to three times a week. People have even gone so far as to plan events and dinner parties simply as an excuse to head down to their local Costco location. Some refuse to vacation in destinations where there isn't a store, because they literally experience physical withdrawal symptoms from not visiting the superstore every few days.

Let's go one step further and move from physical addictions to emotional addictions. I'm sure you've heard of adrenaline addicts. Those crazy individuals who have an intense need to feel a "rush" by defying death in some manner. They can be found participating in extreme sports like cliff-diving or bungee jumping, always looking for the next high. Life seems boring to these men and women unless they are cheating death.

What about the "love addict"? Not to be mistaken for the "sex addict," these are people who jump from relationship to relationship, trying to find the right person to love them perfectly. They often are looking to escape past feelings of abandonment and are using their relationship as an insulator from their own emotions, trying to find self-worth from external sources (Katehakis, 2013). Once the feelings fade from fantastic to fleeting, as they do in every relationship, the love addict will feel compelled to search out the emotion they so desperately desire from a new partner. The flash in the pan will ignite and fade, and the cycle continues.

These are obviously brief overviews of complex emotional struggles that should not be minimized or discounted. But as a society, we have so flippantly thrown around the word "addiction" and thereby have diminished the stigma attached to it. We label things that we merely find pleasurable, and are not necessarily detrimental to our life, as an addiction and have caused it to become socially acceptable.

Chocoholic, anyone?

The fact is, addiction is indicative of something that, to the true sufferer, to the true victim, seems effectually irresistible and insurmountable. The effects of it are demoralizing and destructive. The symptoms become all-consuming, and it seems like literally nothing can alleviate the burden.

The mind is a very intricate structure, but, biblically speaking, it is not a physical one. It houses emotions and thought patterns and memories. What's beautiful about that is we can't physically touch the mind. We can manipulate neurons, and we can stimulate sections of the brain that respond to our thoughts. But ultimately, the mind itself is something that is intangible.

What tends to get us in trouble, though, is not the physical brain cells. Rather, the culprit becomes the pattern of thought that we have allowed ourselves to experience.

For example, take Steve. Steve is a life-of-the-party kind of guy. He has been dating his gorgeous girlfriend for five years and works in a highly competitive, highly paid sales environment. One day, Steve and his girlfriend break up and, suffice it to say, it is not amicable. Understandably, he is deeply hurt. He chooses to drown his sorrows in a couple of beers, and because the pain hasn't gone away for a few weeks, he starts drinking every night. He begins to close off and become emotionally unavailable to all of his friends. He stops answering calls and text messages.

Realizing that he isn't performing well in the workplace, he decides to take a couple of shots before going to work to "take the edge off." Steve begins to feel better and has the best sales day he's had in years. He continues to secretly drink alcohol before work, thinking it's benefitting him. Because his numbers have been in decline, he convinces himself that he needs more and more alcohol to continue to produce.

One day, his boss pulls him into a meeting in his office and questions whether Steve is coming into work drunk. Steve denies everything, until surveillance photos from the underground parking area show him drinking from a bottle in the trunk of his car before coming into the building. Steve is fired on the spot.

Steve has developed his appetite for alcohol through learned behaviors of coping. The chemical balance in his mind responded to, and ultimately was altered by, his thoughts. Although he thought that drinking was benefiting him, he ended up hurting himself. With appetites, when they are fed, they can swell quickly into uncontrollable burdens. Also known as addictions.

Conversely, if appetites are starved, they become weak and manageable, or completely disappear altogether. While easy to say, and far more difficult to do, Steve would need to recognize that the drinking is not benefiting him and stop altogether. The hope is that this realization would come before negative consequences begin to affect him, such as losing his job or worse yet, his life.

Recognizing depressive tendencies can be difficult in the moment. If we take our example of Steve and change the scenario by replacing drinking with another negative behavior more closely related to depression, it might be a bit clearer.

Instead of drinking, let's say that Steve feels that being around his co-workers reminds him of his breakup too much and decides to work from home. Each morning, he wakes up exhausted, unmotivated, and stays in bed all day. He doesn't shower or shave, he never changes out of his pajamas, and instead of working, he binge watches movies. Again, easy to say, but harder to do, Steve needs to recognize that his behavior, in this case depression, is an appetite that can be fed or starved. He needs to decide that giving in to how he feels will negatively affect his life and change his behaviors.

Perhaps, instead of food for thought, it could be said that thought is food…for behavior.

The question that remains unanswered is: how do I change my mindset and behaviors?

Chapter 6

Defense Is…

The Word of God is very clear: anything with a name is cast under the foot of Jesus. He rules all and all are subject to him.

Ephesians 1:20-22
"*[20]Which he wrought in Christ, when he raised him from the dead, and set him at his own right hand in the heavenly places,*

²¹Far above all principality, and power, and might, and dominion, and every name that is named, not only in this world, but also in that which is to come: ²²And <u>hath put all things under his feet</u>, and gave him to be the head over all things to the church,"

Last I checked, *"all things"* includes depression.

Recognizing depression as an identifiable thing removes it from being an ethereal emotion or phenomena. This is an important step in the depressive storm to come. It makes what we are dealing with real or concrete, something that we can work against.

Biblically speaking, depression is known as a spirit of heaviness (*Isaiah 61:3*). For example, I can say that I am tired, want to avoid everyone and spend all day in bed. Or I can recognize that a spirit of heaviness is attacking me. Can you see how much easier it is to address the known thing rather than the fleeting feeling?

Have you ever watched the World Series of Poker? It always struck me as odd why someone would wear crazy hats and sunglasses while playing a card game. I thought it was a mind trick to distract other players from concentrating.

I have since found out that the players are trying to prevent themselves from manifesting a "tell." A tell in poker is an unconscious change in someone's behavior or demeanor that gives clues to that player's hand. If I'm holding a Royal Flush and I start giggling uncontrollably while pushing all my chips into the center, everyone worth their seat at the table will fold, and I won't be able to win as much money.

What do tells have to do with depression? A great deal. In fact, learning your tells when you're about to go into a depressive episode allows you to mount a defense against the coming battle. Think of it like feeling a raindrop on the back of your neck: you know a storm is about to hit. Oftentimes, knowing an attack is coming can mean the difference between victory and defeat.

For instance, I learned that one of my tells is not putting toothpaste on my toothbrush in the morning. (Yeah, I know. Gross. Ever brushed your teeth without toothpaste? Trust me. Don't. Remember I said that depression gets messy?) The point is that for some odd reason, the easy and menial act of putting toothpaste on the toothbrush suddenly became this incredibly difficult, debilitating, and overwhelming exercise. It *felt* insurmountable.

But, truth be told, it was just toothpaste. It took less than a second to do, and it made my mouth and teeth feel significantly better. When I didn't use toothpaste because it was too inundating, I found that I was more readily influenceable by negative thinking and behavior. However, resisting this thought led to me feeling more confident, more valuable, and more capable than I had prior.

Tells come in all shapes and sizes, and taking the time to discover them is a valuable strategy against the enemy. For some, they no longer practice self-care or hygiene. For others, it may be unconsciously utilizing a phrase more regularly, like expressing exhaustion or tiredness. Even an increase in irritability or sudden mood swing could be an indicator. They are usually discovered through experience and are unique to each individual. A good practice would be to write them down in a journal as you discover them. Sometimes memory can be difficult in the midst of struggle.

Recognizing my toothpaste tell as the proverbial calm before the storm helped me realize that I needed a defensive fortification that would repel attacks.

Proverbs 25:28
"He that hath no rule over his own spirit is like a city that is broken down, and without walls."

And thankfully, God had already made all the necessary materials available to mankind.

In the Word of God, there are hundreds of scriptures addressing battles and defensive strategy. One of my favorites is found in Nehemiah 4:17-18, which says:

"¹⁷They which builded on the wall, and they that bare burdens, with those that laded, every one with one of his hands wrought in the work, and with the other hand held a weapon.
¹⁸For the builders, every one had his sword girded by his side, and so builded. And he that sounded the trumpet was by me."

Here we see the Jews rebuilding the wall of Jerusalem after they were released from servitude in Babylon. But the new inhabitants of the land rose up against the Jews and kept attacking, destroying their progress on the wall. So each man resorted to building with one hand and fighting the enemy with the other.

Hallelujah!

Comparing this with the war on depression, you might be seeing strong parallels developing. The enemy keeps attacking and destroying the progress you are making, forcing you to start from the beginning. You feel like you cannot work at your best, like your hands are tied, but the work must continue on your defenses.

Take one step further, though, and examine the bricks in the wall you are building. In this defense against a spiritual enemy, the bricks will not be stone or granite. Instead, they will be scripture.

Isaiah 28:10
"For precept must be upon precept, precept upon precept; line upon line, line upon line; here a little, and there a little:"

Because building your fortification will be much easier when you are not under attack, I encourage you to open your Bible and begin to study passages that encourage you or help you fight against this enemy. Write them down. Keep them in some place that is easily accessible. Each verse will become a brick in your wall, another deterrent to the enemy. Build that wall high, Christian!

My recommendation would be to start in Ephesians Chapter 6, which discusses the Armor of God. There, we understand how we are equipped to fight this spiritual war. If you are unfamiliar with it, feel free to pause here and read the whole chapter. It's *powerful*!

One of the components of the Armor is the sword of the Spirit, which is the Word of God. And in battle, swords are both defensive and offensive. I can deflect blows and strike back in one swing. One of my favorite counterattacks is to arm myself with this scripture:

1 John 3:20-21

"*²⁰For if our heart condemn us, God is greater than our heart, and knoweth all things.*
²¹Beloved, if our heart condemn us not, then have we confidence toward God."

By examining the word *heart* in the scripture above, we see that the word in Greek is "kardia" (G2588). In this context, it means the mind. So if our mind is condemning us, God is greater than our minds! In other words, if I'm thinking that I'm the worst person on the planet or that this situation proves that I am terrible, God is greater than how I think or feel. What does God say about me? How much He loves me? How much He cares for me? How by his death and resurrection I am made new (2 Corinthians 5:17)? How I am renewed in the spirit of my mind, daily (Romans 12:2)?

That scripture, when I wield it, reminds me of who I am in Christ. It firms up my identity and floods my spirit with tons of other scriptures that I can use to fight against the Devil. When God revealed that scripture to me, I was so excited knowing that I was not a slave to how I felt anymore. Rather, I am who God says I am! And then I can remind Satan that he has no power over me. See how quickly the wall was built with bricks of scripture? Glory!

Jumping back to the Armor of God, I want to point out a particular passage that stands out in this war.

> *Ephesians 6:16*
> *"Above all, taking the shield of faith, wherewith ye shall be able to quench all the fiery darts of the wicked."*

Just imagine the sound of a flaming arrow clanging against the steel of a shield. My question to you, dear warrior in Christ, is this: in this battle against depression, what are the fiery darts that you will be able to defend against?

Scripture makes it clear that the weapons of our warfare are not carnal:

> 2 Corinthians 10:4-5
> "⁴(For the weapons of our warfare are <u>not carnal</u>, but mighty through God to the pulling down of strong holds;)
> ⁵Casting down <u>imaginations</u>, and every high thing that exalteth itself against the <u>knowledge</u> of God, and bringing into captivity every <u>thought</u> to the obedience of Christ;"

We can see through the scripture above that the fiery darts mentioned in Ephesians 6 are not physical items. Instead they must be imaginations and thoughts, and they are attacking the principles

God has breathed into us (in this case, we discussed in Chapter 4 that the spirit of heaviness attacks the hope of salvation). The shield of faith is reaching into the future, bringing back the promise of deliverance and victory over Satan, and protecting us in *this* moment!

Glory to God!

So, in the moments when small, counterproductive thoughts that have led to downward spirals in the past invade your mind, you can recognize them as tells. And work against them!

Thoughts of staying in bed all day. Thoughts that people don't like you. Thoughts of worthlessness. Thoughts of hopelessness. Thoughts of self-condemnation.

These are all fiery darts of the wicked that have made it past your armor and have struck you. They are speaking against the work that God has done in you, like poison in the mind, trying to convince you that you don't matter. Stirring up emotions in the hopes that you will act upon them negatively. Warrior of Christ, this is the battle you are in. But it's not over.

You've only begun to fight!

Chapter 7

Thought Is…

H ave you seen the Pixar movie *Inside Out*? It is a beautiful allegory for the carnal mind. Emotions like Joy and Anger are running the daily operations, making decisions, collecting and protecting core memories that impact self worth and values. Society has determined that how we feel must automatically dictate how we act. I am sad, therefore I cry. I'm angry, therefore I shout or break things.

But the mind of a Christian is no longer defined by carnality. Instead the Christian mind is spiritually transformed.

> *Romans 8:6-8*
> "⁶*For to be carnally minded is death; but to be* ***spiritually minded is life and peace.***
> ⁷*Because the carnal mind is enmity against God: for it is not subject to the law of God, neither indeed can be.*
> ⁸*So then they that are in the flesh cannot please God."*

Because Christ is now Lord over you, the way you process emotions and thoughts must change. Within scripture, we constantly see the universal word *heart* used to describe the spiritual inner workings of man: the mind, the spirit, the soul. But expounding and defining the words in the Bible, as we did in our earlier example of God being greater than our minds, will help reveal another strategy to fighting this war:

You are not your thoughts.

I know what you're thinking. Those who are scripturally versed will go directly to this scripture to argue against this point:

Proverbs 23:7a
"For as he thinketh in his heart, so is he:"

But look up the word *heart* in that scripture and you will find the Hebrew word "nephesh"(H5315), which means *soul*.

In other words, as you think in your soul, so are you. And this becomes important in the battle against depression. We must define and recognize the difference between thoughts of the mind and thoughts of the soul.

Shonda Moralis in her online article made this statement: "Our beliefs are powerful in that we unknowingly morph thoughts into facts" (2019). When thought enters the mind, it is simply that – a thought. It may be true; it may not. But mankind has a tendency, when overwhelmed, to transform notion into fact, no matter how it is presented. It's just easier to submit to the thought rather than fight against it. This is a major tactic of Satan and the spirit of heaviness.

God has given us the mind as the vessel to process thought. But the mind is not the final destination. Think of a thought in the mind like a peach pit clanging around inside a sealed coffee can. There is no soil for the seed to root in, so it seeks where it can grow by clanking against the sides of the can.

The more the pit clangs, the more intense the sound, and the more one feels the pressure of needing to address it with immediacy.

For most, the process of calming the mind and processing that thought is innate. They are able to extract and examine the thought with relative ease.

But imagine adding a dozen more seeds, all clanging around in the coffee can alongside each other. The pits are bouncing around so violently that they are shattering into smaller pieces, each shard a new complex thought.

With all these thoughts wreaking havoc and multiplying stress in the mind, the need to accept or reject thoughts with impetuousness becomes amplified. But with all that chaos, trying to pick out just one piece to weigh its merits and benefits feels impossible and not worth the effort.

It's easy to see how overwhelmed one can get. It often leaves the thinker trying to do all they can to *make it stop!* Entering a damage-control process, they begin flippantly accepting or rejecting thoughts without regard to detriment, actively searching for a moment of peace to make some sense of anything and everything. This is commonly referred to as anxiety, which, when combined with depressive tendencies, can be extremely difficult to work through.

I cannot emphasize enough how important it is to find someone to help you filter through the peach pits. But not just any stranger on the street will do. Whether it's your pastor, or a qualified biblical counselor, or even a strong Christian friend, find someone you are willing to be vulnerable with and who will help you work through your thoughts towards a stronger faith in Jesus Christ.

Sometimes, either due to the way we were raised or other life circumstances, we are left unaware of the God-given tools we possess to properly process what is happening in our minds. There is no shame in admitting you do not have the resources. But pretending you do can be harmful. Make sure you share your ideas and feelings, and make sure you are sharing with the right person on a regular basis. Think of sharing like the mortar between the bricks of scripture in the wall of your fortification. It's going to take some extra work, but it will make your wall that much more impenetrable.

Turning back to the thought, for all of its clanging, it must have something to facilitate it from seed to tree, from abstract into reality. In scripture, land is used metaphorically as the physical representation of what happens in our inner man. Simply put, we sow something, and we reap the fruit of that seed.

When a thought is processed and accepted as truth, it transitions down into the soul, where it will begin to influence and direct action, very much like the core memories in *Inside Out*. After the thought takes root, it will till up any remaining fallow ground that it can, thereby preparing for other similar thoughts to be more easily accepted. Thus, future action will be affected with greater propensity. This is why it is so imperative to address and confirm all thought before it is sown into the depths of the heart.

Proverbs 4:23
"Keep thy heart with all diligence; for out of it are the issues of life."

The word *heart* there in Hebrew is "leb" (H3820), which means the *mind* or *understanding*, further reinforcing how important this battle is.

Let me give a neutral, and yet unequivocally polarizing, example.

Imagine thinking, *I like pineapple on pizza.*

It's an argument for the ages. If somehow you haven't heard, a quick Google search will help affirm how many people hold *very* strong opinions on it. And more than likely, you have already made up your mind on this subject. But that's the point. In your mind is where you challenge the veracity of thought.

In our example, to confirm that you like Hawaiian pizza, you pick up a piping hot slice, take a bite of it, and...fireworks explode in your mouth. It's amazing! Soft, chewy, sweet, savory, delicious! You accept the thought as true, and then it descends into your soul where it will be planted and bear fruit, causing you to seek out Hawaiian pizza at every pool party and large gathering you attend ever again.

But what if the fireworks didn't explode? What if you hated it? The slimy, shrivelly, pineapple clashed horribly with the salty cheese and acidic marinara. You'd disagree with the thought, *I like pineapple on pizza* and cast it out of your mind, where it cannot take root in your soul.

And while liking Hawaiian pizza is hardly a life-altering thought, it shows how we process thoughts of the mind. Replacing menial thoughts of preference with weightier ones like self-worth and belief systems raises the stakes.

God clearly states that the storm we are silencing is not a carnal, fleshly one. Unlike war, punches and bombs and assault rifles have no effect. As we learned earlier, Satan isn't launching physical arrows that have been set ablaze. These arrows are thoughts that will burn in the mind, imaginations that are purposed to steal, kill, and destroy hope and faith. Hence why we must bring into captivity *every thought* (2 *Corinthians* 10:5) to determine whether it will help us or hurt us, whether it is from God or an attempt at espionage by the enemy. Truly, then, the mind is our battlefield! But this is what the Lord has to say about that:

2 *Chronicles 20:15*
"And he said, Hearken ye, all Judah, and ye inhabitants of Jerusalem, and thou king Jehoshaphat, Thus saith the LORD unto you, Be not afraid nor dismayed by reason of this great multitude; <u>for the battle is not yours, but God's</u>."

The mind is the battlefield, and because you belong to Christ, the battle is His. And just in case you don't know or somehow forgot during the battle,

God *always* wins the war. Remember: you are not your thoughts. Not every thought you think comes from you, is true, or even beneficial to you.

But how can we determine if a thought is worth planting in our soul? How can we prevent ourselves from being overwhelmed by the enemy and accepting a negative thought?

Chapter 8

Cheese Is…

If you have experienced repetitive intrusive thoughts, which are spontaneous, unwanted ideas, you know how seemingly unending that can feel. What you are discovering spiritually is that the enemy has found a hole in your armor and is striking it, over and over and over again.

If you are feeling depressed, the spirit of heaviness is the source of those repetitive strikes.

Oftentimes for me, these arrows are accusations against my character or reminders of traumatic events, small or large. But no matter how many times you get hit, no matter how many drops of rain crash down on you, the truth does not change. It is still the enemy trying to lie to you. You are still a child of God. And God is still not done equipping you with methods to be victorious in this war.

After you have determined tells of oncoming attacks, fortified your defensive position in scripture, and recognized that you are not your thoughts, the next step is to make your stand.

> *Ephesians 6:13*
> *"Wherefore take unto you the whole armour of God, that ye may be able to withstand in the evil day, and having done all, <u>to stand</u>."*

For several years, I was given the opportunity to serve as the safety coordinator for an aviation company. As you may know, aviation is considered the safest form of travel available to mankind. And there is perfectly sound justification for that. Immense labor and financial resources have been committed to mitigating, or possibly eliminating, as much risk as possible in all phases of flight. Obviously, if the powers that be wanted to be completely safe in aviation and effectively reduce risk to zero, flight would stop altogether. But that is not feasible in this fast-paced world.

There is a particularly famous safety model that, if you have ever worked in or around a safety-dependent environment, would be very familiar to you. It is known as the Swiss Cheese Model of Accident Causation, developed by James T. Reason, et al (2000). In times of processing incidents that produced overwhelming quantities of data, and evidence, and emotions (yes, even the safety guys have feelings), I came to appreciate the simplicity it provided.

This model has been used across the globe to give insight into how an accident may have occurred. It uses categories such as company policy, human factors, culture, or other organizational factors, and displays them as slices of swiss cheese, that *should* prevent and defend against an accident occurring.

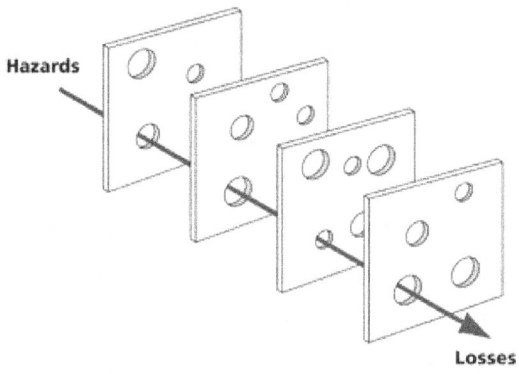

Figure 1 – Swiss Cheese Model of Accident Causation

But, just like swiss cheese, each category has its own unique set of holes in it. If the slices line up just right, the trajectory of a hazard can pass right through the slices and turn into an incident or loss. It gives a tangible way of thinking about how the policies and procedures businesses have in place can appear to be whole on the outside, but are really laden with gaps that can cause loss.

It is impossible to know the number of accidents prevented by these models, and whether it completely eliminates the shortcomings. But it certainly has allowed the aviation community to see that we can fly millions of miles and millions of passengers every year all across the globe with a relatively miniscule amount of risk.

That same swiss cheese methodology can be applied to other areas of life, including the modes of thinking we engage in. If we take the negative thoughts that are rising up within our minds (hazards), and we use a series of questions (slices) to challenge or defend against these hazards, then there would theoretically be limited or no incidents or losses (spiral into depression, negative behavior, etc).

I remember distinctly when God began forming this concept into a tangible reality. Driving home from work on a Friday evening on the freeway overpass, rush-hour traffic honking all around me, a thought pierced into my consciousness without warning. It seemed small and insignificant, but I've learned that when those take root, they grow with haste and vitriol.

"I'm so stupid. Remember that time four years ago in church where I said ABC and everyone completely ignored me? I'm an idiot."

That statement is a dangerous one. It wasn't uncommon for me to have thoughts like that, but that particular moment on that bridge resonated with me. Miraculously, God intervened in that moment and caused me to resist what would normally be the beginning of a very detrimental downward spiral.

Rather than accept the thought as truth, instead of succumbing to the pressure of the moment and allowing it to take root in my soul, God questioned it for me. In that still small voice, He asked me if I could declare, without a doubt, that people were still mocking me because of that scenario. And I began to realize what was happening.

I was completely alone in my car, so this intrusive thought didn't come from someone else, thereby ruling out human influence. Even in the weeks afterwards, no one from the church had said anything about it. And here we were, four years later, without a single mention of it to me. Which led me to two possible sources of the thought: God or Satan. Because I know that to be spiritually minded will bring peace (*Romans 8:6*), I could rule out God being the source of such a tormentive thought. Clearly, it was a fiery dart of the wicked that had made it through my armor!

So, I chose to acknowledge that the statement was not true. God urged me to go one step further and ask myself this: if someone was theoretically making fun of me, was I allowed to make mistakes? I had to sheepishly admit and remind myself that I, as a human, am error-prone. Mistakes happen. Even if someone was making fun of me, they were wrong, and immature for doing it so many years later.

I began to accept that what I spoke at church was not nearly as detrimental or impactful as the thought had implied. These two simple yet challenging questions gave me the freedom and strength to pluck out (or reject) the fiery dart that Satan had struck me with. What I said was, at worst, incorrect. It wasn't sinful or worthy of condemnation. I was not a horrible person because of the trivial mistake I made so long ago.

Rather, it was Satan trying to use that incident to undermine my strength and faith in Christ. In order to fight against this seed and to show that I was unashamed of the transformation I was undergoing, I shared this testimony at a Bible study later that same night. A few attendees that evening had been at the church four years ago, so I asked their thoughts on the matter.

Not one of them remembered that moment in time. Satan truly is the accuser of the brethren (*Revelations 12:9-10*)!

This revelation led to the development of what I am calling the Swiss Cheese Model of Thinking, which we'll go over in more depth in the next chapter.

Chapter 9

The W.E.S.T. Is…

The Swiss Cheese Model of Thinking consists of four categories to filter through when fighting against the hazardous thoughts that seemingly pop up out of nowhere.

Again, as we learned before, we cannot merely accept all thought as fact and truth. We must challenge its veracity and assess its viability before we plant it in our soul.

As we delve deeper into this revelation, it should become clearer to you that the sun is setting on Satan's reign in your life!

Praise the Lord!

And where does the sun set? In the acronym W.E.S.T.

Each letter represents an easily performed cognitive concept designed to combat the fiery darts of the wicked. The letters in W.E.S.T. will represent our four proverbial cheese slices that, when used in conjunction with each other, will concisely funnel thoughts for processing whether to accept or reject it. Let's break each letter down.

W. WORD OF GOD

E. EMOTIONS

S. SCHEMA

T. TRUTH

WORD OF GOD. Does the thought line up with God's Word? Is this a promise that God has made or not? Can you substantiate or disprove what is going on in your scenario with scripture? Open your Bible and physically find it in the Word. Since the mind is our battlefield, we cannot trust our minds to remember everything correctly during the chaos. This is the premier filter and the best way to know whether the thought you are experiencing is of God or if you should reject it.

EMOTIONS. Are emotions affecting your perception of the situation? Is anger, loneliness, etc. either aggrandizing or minimizing how serious the situation is? Because they are so volatile and impactful, Satan uses emotion to elicit responses from people that they would not normally produce.

Not all emotion is bad. But this is usually a great indicator that Satan is attempting to move you from a place of peace to a place of turmoil. If emotion is present, do not make decisions about the present scenario. If possible, wait for the feelings to pass before making final judgments.

SCHEMA. This word is Greek for *mind path*. These are defense mechanisms the brain utilizes to protect itself from perceived threats. These prescribed series of behaviors or thought patterns often have destructive consequences and are sometimes difficult to recognize in the midst of them.

Once the mind begins the path, it can be very strenuous to stop midstream. You may even find yourself asking why you are doing what you are doing. You may feel like you want to do something else but are unable, instead continuing down the same path, ad nauseum. If you have ever found yourself in similar situations repeatedly and negatively responding the exact same way without thinking about it, it is probably a schema.

Utilize these questions to challenge the thought: Have you been in this scenario before? How did you respond? Was it how you wanted to respond? Could you do it better?

These are tough questions to ask during a mind trial, so try to think of how you would like to respond before you are in a struggle. As scripture declares in 2 Corinthians 13:5, examine yourself. Determine scenarios you have been in that have clearly caused you to manifest schemas and discover better ways to deal with them. Speak with your pastor or a qualified biblical counselor if you need help in this area.

TRUTH. Is the information in the thought verifiable? Or are you willingly accepting a lie because it is easier than trying to deal with the thought? Satan deals in half-truths. Like putting lipstick on a pig or lacing sugar with cyanide, he will wrap lies in thin coatings of truth so that they appear more beautiful and are more easily received. Think objectively here. The truth hurts, but being deceived and discovering it later hurts more. Honesty with yourself will be a key factor in this filter. Pray that the Holy Spirit will guide you into all truth (*John 16:13*).

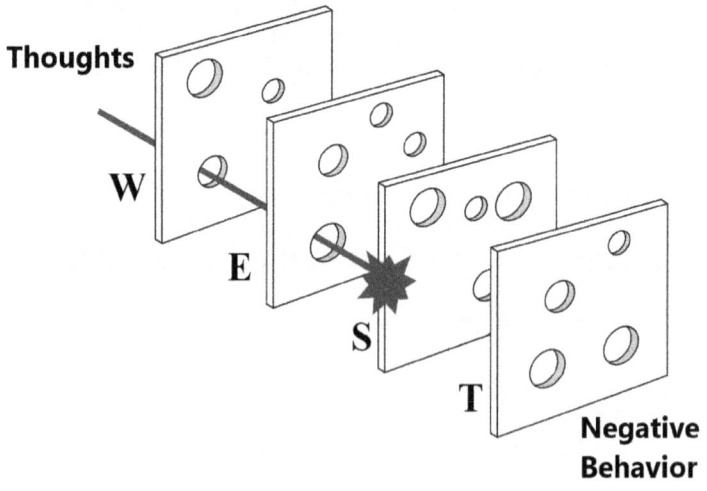

Figure 2 – Swiss Cheese Model of Thinking in application.

Let's utilize that information by applying the W.E.S.T. acronym to the statement I shared before.

"I'm so stupid. Remember that time four years ago in church where I said ABC and everyone completely ignored me? I'm an idiot."

WORD OF GOD. Scripture declares that we as Christians have been given the mind of Christ (*1 Corinthians 2:16*). Is Christ stupid? Of course not. He is God, creator of logic and intelligence. He is omniscient, or all-knowing. There are examples of people in scripture being called foolish or churlish, such as Nabal (*1 Samuel 25:3*). However, these were wicked people who opposed God. And as a Christian, you stand with God, not against Him. You stand for the opposite of wickedness: holiness. So, with the very first sentence, we can already reject the fiery dart right from the beginning.

RESULT: Reject the thought.

For the sake of exercise, let's walk through the rest.

EMOTIONS. When the words fell out of my mouth and everyone in the church ignored me, I immediately felt regret for having spoken it. (Also read: *insert foot in mouth here*). But to experience the same regret four years later over something that did not warrant that emotional response in the first place is indicative of something out of order. Either I have not forgiven myself and resolved the issue emotionally, or Satan is slinging arrows and thoughts of my past into me in order to see what causes me to emote. And, let's be honest, it could be both.

No matter the cause, the negative emotional response is indicative that the thought I am experiencing is suspect. When God speaks, even in times of correction, there should be a sense of peace and resolve around how to move into reconciliation with Christ. In other words, if I am wrong, God will show me how to return to Him and give me the ability to do it. The emotion I experienced on the drive home did not produce peace or resolve. Unaddressed, I would have felt worthless and spiraled into incapability. This is clearly grounds for rejection of the thought.

RESULT: Reject the thought.

SCHEMA. I have experienced thoughts like this in the past. In the interest of transparency (as if this whole book isn't a detailed description of personal candor), I usually accepted these thoughts without consideration. I didn't realize that I was accepting them or that I even *could* reject them. The thought just *was*. I trusted my mind to tell me only the truth. What a detrimental approach! This thought was like all the other negative ones and would lead into a worldview of negativity and depression. Because of those past incidents, I can recognize that this is going to lead me into a schema that I have no desire to participate in.

RESULT: Reject the thought.

TRUTH. This is where God took me from the outset. I believe this was because I was not in the correct frame of mind to challenge the thought using the previous methods. Regardless, at that moment, I could not verify that people were still mocking me. Therefore, shame and regret were not feasible emotional responses to something that might not be true. It was too soon to react in that manner. And as I shared before, after speaking to individuals who were there, they didn't even remember the incident. My negative emotional response would have been unwarranted and unnecessary.

RESULT: Reject the thought.

Clearly, every slice of cheese in the example above would have filtered out the thought and stopped me from accepting it.

Let's try another one.

"I am just a burden to everyone around me."

Sound familiar? It is an exceptionally common thought to those who have suffered from or are currently experiencing depression. There is nothing new under the sun (*Ecclesiastes 1:9*). Let's set the sun on this one.

WORD OF GOD. The Devil is a liar and the father thereof (*John 8:44*)! I've said that statement of feeling like a burden, both in my head and out loud, more times than I care to admit. And the shameful stigma carried by that thought has caused countless people to spiral into depression. But what does the Word of God say?

1 Peter 5:7
"Casting all your care upon him; for he careth for you."

Matthew 11:28-30
"²⁸ Come unto me, all ye that labour and are heavy laden, and I will give you rest.
²⁹ Take my yoke upon you, and learn of me; for I am meek and lowly in heart: and ye shall find rest unto your souls.
³⁰ For my yoke is easy, and my burden is light."

These are just two of many scriptures that show God understands and expects us to go through trial and tribulation. Why else would He give these scriptures to us, inviting us to come to Him when we are heavy laden? Friend, it's not wrong to be a burden.

Galatians 6:2
"Bear ye one another's burdens, and so fulfil the law of Christ."

Look at it this way: someone has to be a burden for others to bear and thus fulfill the law of Christ. But the followers of Jesus must not allow themselves to stay in that place. They must find a way to come out from beneath that weight of burden and serve others in Christ.

Take the parable of the Good Samaritan in Luke 10:30-37. The Good Samaritan bore the responsibility of caring for a complete stranger, and a Jew at that. When Jesus was giving this parable, Samaritans and Jews were not even allowed to walk on the same road simultaneously. They lived in separate communities and even worshiped God differently. So, how is it that the Good Samaritan paid for the room and board at the inn for that injured Jew and even stated he would pay any other balance when he returns? Is it safe to say that the Good Samaritan recognized the inherent value of the injured man more than what society told him he should? We all will be burdensome at some time or another. And God always provides a way of escape (*1 Corinthians 10:13*).

RESULT: Reject the thought.

EMOTION. This thought of feeling like a burden is drenched in emotion. Rejection. Anger. Fear. Frustration. Exhaustion. Wanting to give up. There are more and varied feelings for each individual, to be sure. Definitely refrain from accepting this notion as truth.

RESULT: Reject the thought.

SCHEMA. When this thought enters my mind, based on prior experience, I know that the next behavior is going to be to withdraw myself from those who I think I am burdening. I do not want to be a burden to anyone. But I really want to not feel this way, which requires me to let others know how I am feeling.

Seeking help is not a burden. If someone sought my help, I would not hesitate to offer what I can. Therefore, I can reasonably believe that others feel the same. And while I may have experienced negative reactions from those closest to me in the past, that does not mean that no one on the planet is willing to help me. This prescribed set of behaviors, the withdrawing from people, will negatively reinforce my state of mind. Therefore, the conclusion is obvious.

RESULT: Reject the thought.

TRUTH. The first three words of the statement affirms the depressive state of the person by minimizing their identity: "I am just..." It is reinforcing their worldview of self as being without value. But is it true? Can I prove that I am a burden to every single person? Have I asked friends, family, my church and others around me? Have I asked God if I am a burden to Him? If you have read the previous chapters, you know that *you are valuable*, even in a burdensome state. You are still loved, which means you are not truly a burden.

RESULT: Reject the thought.

Let's do one more. What about a thought that isn't so cut and dried? Maybe something that is innocuous or less obvious, like a "tell"?

"I'm just tired."

WORD OF GOD. Matthew 11:28-30 shows that it is okay to be tired, feeling weary and heavy laden. God does not command me to be strong all day, every day.

RESULT: Continue to challenge the thought.

EMOTIONS. Why do I feel tired? Am I physically exhausted from a long day's work? Am I emotionally drained or mentally taxed from a difficult day at work? Did someone do something that hurt me recently and am I using the feeling of being tired as a cover for my pain? Or is the spirit of heaviness weighing on me?

In this scenario, let's say that it was a tough day at work and you just need a few hours alone. Self-care is a vital part of fighting against the enemy because it reinforces value. That is a perfectly acceptable and necessary behavior.

RESULT: Continue to challenge the thought.

SCHEMA. When I have used that sentence in the past, it was a secret phrase I used to confirm what I wanted to feel. It indicated that I was overwhelmed and that whatever thought pattern I was experiencing was one that I did not want to participate in. In other words, it was a tell about what might come. It would encourage those few needed hours alone. But then my flesh would step in, turning hours into days or even weeks lacking motivation and desiring to stay in bed. It would become a circle of avoidance. Can you see the schema? You have probably experienced this thought before, and you know what will happen if you simply accept it as being a minimally impactive thought or temporary experience.

RESULT: Reject the thought.

TRUTH. We already rejected the thought in the Schema section, so no need to continue challenging it.

Ultimately, the goal of the Swiss Cheese Model of Thinking is to provide you with not just a coping mechanism for struggle, but to challenge thought patterns and indicators (appetites) before they become struggles (depression). Challenging thought patterns like this is not easy, especially under the weight and lack of motivation that comes from feeling depressed.

At least, not at first.

Time and time again, this model has proven effective in keeping thoughts from turning into incidents, losses, or depressive episodes. I've learned the more I use it, the more intuitive it becomes. And the more intuitive it becomes, the faster I am able to reject those negative thoughts before they clang against the sides of the coffee can or manage to take root in my soul.

Soldier in Christ, let me be candid with you: there will be times where you will face a continual barrage of fiery darts from the enemy. The arrows may be so great in number that the skies of your life turn dark, and it may feel like it will never end.

Moments like those remind me of a movie in which the main character is swarmed by bats. As he cowers under the immensity of the moment, it is clear that it is an allegory for being consumed by fear. The man returns after several years to face his greatest horror, standing unflinchingly in the midst of a whirlwind of winged creatures. Later, he utilizes the thing he feared most as a symbol of provoking dread in others.

But as Christians, we don't defeat the Devil using the power of the Devil (*Luke 11:18*). We cast out devils by the Word of God!

Pick an arrow, pick a thought, and silence it! One by one, until there are none left. Do not stop. Do not surrender.

We are empowered to stop the enemy's attack in its tracks and prevent hazardous thoughts from becoming incidents of depression in the same manner that Jesus calmed the storm.

Mark 4:39:
"And he arose, and rebuked the wind, and said unto the sea, Peace, be still. And the wind ceased, and there was a great calm."

Tells, like raindrops, will stand out as obvious signs of a larger upcoming attack, and you will have the necessary tools at your disposal to defeat the enemy.

On the last page of this book, there is a small, business-card-sized tool to help you practice walking through the W.E.S.T. process. I call it the Storm Breaker's Quick Card. Feel free to cut it out. It's perfect for the wallet or purse, so it will be easily accessible. I laminated the one in my wallet so that it would last longer.

Chapter 10

Victory Is…

Victory. Now I have victory.

That is written in sharp contrast to the opening line of the book where I shared that the most I could muster up was a request for relief.

I pray, in the name of Jesus Christ, you can see how far apart desiring relief and experiencing victory exists from one another, that you can see the miraculous journey towards understanding God brought me through, using His Word. I pray, also, that you see that victory is available for you as well.

We have discussed important concepts, such as how appetites are developed and ways depression manifests. We have discovered how thoughts are like peach pits in tin cans. We have delved into deep contemplation in spiritual warfare, how faith and hope and charity affect our salvation, and ultimately, how we interact with God. We have gone so far as to dissect the difference between thoughts of the mind and thoughts of the soul. And we have brought to light some of the secret tactics of Satan, how he is attacking believers and unbelievers alike with a spirit of heaviness.

But my earnest desire is that these concepts help you understand that by the power of Jesus Christ, you are more than a conqueror (*Romans 8:37*) —

that you also are a Storm Breaker, calming the storm of depression in your mind (*Mark 4:39*).

Satan is the real enemy. Working the precepts in this book *will* help you defeat him. And while these principles are aimed at depression, they are most certainly empowered by God in every area of spiritual warfare: lust, anger, judgment, hatred, etc.

> *Deuteronomy 20:4*
> *"For the LORD your God is he that goeth with you, to fight for you against your enemies, to save you."*

There is no greater power than Jesus Christ. It's in His name that we become victorious. And that freedom... Oh, that sweet, sweet freedom! To think clearly, stand in faith, and walk with the Lord is worth enduring any sacrifice.

Fight for that freedom! Victory is yours through Jesus! Remember, the sun is *setting* on Satan's reign in your life. And where does the sun set?

In the W.E.S.T.!

Works Cited

1. World Health Organization. (2021, September 13). *Depression.* WHO | World Health Organization. Retrieved February 23, 2022, from https://www.who.int/news-room/fact-sheets/detail/depression

2. American Psychiatric Association. (2013). *DSM Library.* Psychiatry Online | DSM Library. Retrieved September 29, 2019, from https://doi.org/10.1176/appi.books.9780890425596

3. Efthimiou, A. (2019, July 5). *Does the DSM Over-Medicalize Human Emotions?* The Mighty. Retrieved February 23, 2020, from https://themighty.com/2019/07/modern-psychiatry-over-medicalization-mental-illnesses/

4. Juergens, J. (2021, October 4). *Antidepressant addiction and abuse.* Addiction Center. Retrieved January 18, 2022, from https://www.addictioncenter.com/stimulants/antidepressants/

5. Lewis, R. (2016, January 26). *"Costcoholics" Costco's $113.7 Billion Addicts.* - The Robin Report. Retrieved September 19, 2019, from https://www.therobinreport.com/costcoholics-costcos-113-7-billion-addicts/

6. Katehakis, A. (2013, May 26). *What is Love Addiction?* Psych Central. Retrieved November 18, 2019, from https://psychcentral.com/blog/what-is-love-addiction#1

7. Moralis, S. (2019, October 3). *I've Been a Therapist For 24 Years – and This Is What I Learned About Those Who Say "I Hate People"*. CNBC. Retrieved November 15, 2019, from https://www.cnbc.com/2019/10/03/therapist-shares-what-she-learned-about-those-who-say-i-hate-people.html

8. Reason, J. (2000, March 18). *Human error: models and management*. NCBI. Retrieved October 7, 2019, from https://www.ncbi.nlm.nih.gov/pmc/articles/PMC1117770/

9. Whitaker, R. (2010, November 1). *New rat study: SSRI's markedly deplete brain serotonin*. Psychology Today. Retrieved February 18, 2022, from https://www.psychologytoday.com/us/blog/mad-in-america/201011/new-rat-study-ssris-markedly-deplete-brain-serotonin

Storm Breaker's Quick Card

WORD
What does scripture say? Do your thoughts line up?

EMOTION
Are emotions aggrandizing or minimizing the situation?

SCHEMA
Mind Path. Is prior trauma affecting this situation?

TRUTH
Is the information verifiable? Can you prove it?

WORD
What does scripture say? Do your thoughts line up?

EMOTION
Are emotions aggrandizing or minimizing the situation?

SCHEMA
Mind Path. Is prior trauma affecting this situation?

TRUTH
Is the information verifiable? Can you prove it?

1 John 3:20-21 "20For if our heart condemn us, God is greater than our heart, and knoweth all things. 21 Beloved, if our heart condemn us not, then have we confidence toward God."
Ephesians 6:16 "Above all, taking the shield of faith, wherewith ye shall be able to quench all the fiery darts of the wicked."
2 Timothy 1:7 "For God hath not given us the spirit of fear; but of power, and of love, and of a sound mind."
Romans 12:2 "And be not conformed to this world: but be ye transformed by the renewing of your mind, that ye may prove what is that good, and acceptable, and perfect, will of God."
Isaiah 41:10 "Fear thou not; for I am with thee: be not dismayed; for I am thy God: I will strengthen thee; yea, I will help thee; yea, I will uphold thee with the right hand of my righteousness."

1 John 3:20-21 "20For if our heart condemn us, God is greater than our heart, and knoweth all things. 21 Beloved, if our heart condemn us not, then have we confidence toward God."
Ephesians 6:16 "Above all, taking the shield of faith, wherewith ye shall be able to quench all the fiery darts of the wicked."
2 Timothy 1:7 "For God hath not given us the spirit of fear; but of power, and of love, and of a sound mind."
Romans 12:2 "And be not conformed to this world: but be ye transformed by the renewing of your mind, that ye may prove what is that good, and acceptable, and perfect, will of God."
Isaiah 41:10 "Fear thou not; for I am with thee: be not dismayed; for I am thy God: I will strengthen thee; yea, I will help thee; yea, I will uphold thee with the right hand of my righteousness."

www.ingramcontent.com/pod-product-compliance
Lightning Source LLC
Chambersburg PA
CBHW060325050426
42449CB00011B/2663